Be Wings of Love

Poems of encouragement and blessing

Compiled by
RICKY MCCOUBREY

CRIMOND
HOUSE

CRIMOND HOUSE PUBLICATIONS

Published in 2020 by
Crimond House Publications
A division of
Ards Evangelical Bookshop
"Crimond House"
48 Frances Street
Newtownards
Co. Down
BT23 7DN
www.ardsbookshop.com

Typesetting and cover design by Crimond House
Publications.

ISBN: 978 1 908618 27 6

Afraid of What?

Afraid? Of what?
To feel the spirit's glad release?
To pass from pain to perfect peace,
The strife and strain of life to cease?
Afraid? Of that?

Afraid? Of what?
Afraid to see the Saviour's face,
To hear His welcome, and to trace,
The glory gleam from wounds of grace,
Afraid? Of that?

Afraid? Of what?
A flash – a crash – a pierced heart;
Brief darkness – Light – O Heaven's art!
A wound of His a counterpart!
Afraid? Of that?

Afraid? Of what?
To enter into Heaven's rest,
And yet to serve the Master blessed?
From service good to service best?
Afraid? Of that?

Afraid? Of what?
To do by death what life could not –
Baptise with blood a stony plot,
Till souls shall blossom from that spot?
Afraid? Of that?

E.H. HAMILTON*

> * Mr. Hamilton heard of the martyrdom of a fellow-
> missionary. As he faced execution, he was asked "Are
> you afraid?". He replied, "No. If you shoot, I go
> straight to heaven." On hearing of the incident, he
> wrote this poem.

A Little Farther

Just before His trial, Jesus entered dark
Gethsemane;
Leaving eight outside, took Peter and two sons of
Zebedee.
Oh, the anguish in the garden, as again He left the
three;
And He went a little farther, all the way to Calvary!

See Him praying, hear Him groaning; death
sweeps o'er Him like a flood;
"Let this cup pass from me, Father"—sweat runs
down as drops of blood!
"Not my will, Lord, I will drink it: let Thy will be
done in Me."
And He went a little farther, all the way to Calvary!

Then at Pilate's hall, behold Him, as the mob who
mocked Him cried,
"Away, away, give us Barabbas; let this Christ be
crucified!"
O Barabbas, O Barabbas, Jesus surely died for thee,
When He went a little farther, all the way to
Calvary!

Now He marches to Golgotha, scourged and
thorn-crowned on the road;
Bears the cross upon His shoulder, sinks beneath
the heavy load!
Mocked, reviled, by friends forsaken—all for you,
and all for me—
And He went a little farther, all the way to Calvary!

Let us go a little farther, farther than we've gone
before;
Are we workers now for Jesus? Let us do a little
more.

AUTHOR UNKNOWN

A Little Talk With Jesus

A little talk with Jesus,
How it smooths the rugged road!
How it seems to help me onward,
When I faint beneath my load;
When my heart is crushed with sorrow,
And my eyes with tears are dim,
There is naught can yield me comfort
Like a little talk with Him.

I tell Him I am weary,
And I fain would be at rest,
That I'm daily, hourly longing
For a home upon His breast!
And He answers me so sweetly,
In tones of tenderest love
I am coming soon to take thee
To my happy home above.

Ah, this is what I'm wanting,
His lovely face to see;
And I'm not afraid to say it,
I know He's wanting me.
He gave His life a ransom,
To make me all His own,
And He'll ne'er forget His promise
To me, His purchased one.

I cannot live without Him,
Nor would I if I could;
He is my daily portion,
My comforter and food.
He is altogether lovely;
None can with Him compare;
The chiefest of ten thousand,
And fairest of the fair.

I often feel impatient,
And mourn His long delay;
I never can be settled
While He remains away–,
But we shall not long be parted,
For I know He'll quickly come,
And we shall dwell together
In that happy, happy home.

So I'll wait a little longer,
Till His appointed time,
And along the upward pathway,
My pilgrim feet shall climb.
There, in my Father's dwelling,
Where many mansions be,
I shall sweetly talk with Jesus,
And He will talk with me.

Fanny J. Crosby

All Ye That Pass By

All ye that pass by,
To Jesus draw nigh:
To you it is nothing that Jesus should die?
Your ransom and peace,
Your surety He is;
Come, see if there ever was sorrow like His.

He dies to atone
For sins not His own;
Your debt He hath paid, and your work He hath
done.
Ye all may receive
The peace He did leave,
Who made intercession, "My Father, forgive!"

For you and for me,
He prayed on the tree;
The prayer is accepted, the sinner is free.
That sinner am I,
Who on Jesus rely,
And come for the pardon God cannot deny.

My pardon I claim,
A sinner I am, —
A sinner believing in Jesus Christ's name.
He purchased the grace
Which now I embrace:
O Father, Thou know'st He hath died in my place.

CHARLES WESLEY

Amazement at the Incarnation of God

To spread the azure canopy of heaven,
And make it twinkle with those spangs of gold,
To stay this weighty mass of earth so even,
That it should all, and nought should it uphold;
To give strange motions to the planets seven,
Or Jove to make so meek, or Mars so bold,
To temper what is moist, dry, hot, and cold,
Of all their jars that sweet accords are given,
Lord, to thy wisdom nought is, nor thy might
But that thou shouldst, Thy glory laid aside,
Come meanly in mortality to bide,
And die for those deserved eternal plight,
A wonder is so far above our wit,
That angels stand amazed to muse on it.

WILLIAM DRUMMOND

Are All the Children In?

I think of times as the night draws nigh
Of an old house on the hill,
Of a yard all wide and blossom-starred
Where the children played at will.

And when the deep night at last came down,
Hushing the merry din,
Mother would look all around and ask,
"Are all the children in?"

'Tis many and many a year since then,
And the old house on the hill
No longer echoes childish feet
And the yard is still, so still.

But I see it all as the shadows creep,
And tho' many the years have been
Since then, I can hear my mother ask,
"Are all the children in?"

I wonder if, when those shadows fall
On the last short earthly day
When we say goodbye to earth —
To its pain its work its play

When we step across the river
Where mother so long has been
Will we hear her ask the final time
"Are all the children in"?

Florence Jones Hadley

Beneath an eastern sky

Beneath an eastern sky,
Amid a rabble's cry,
A Man went forth to die
For me.

Thorn-crowned His lovely head,
Blood-stained His every tread;
Cross-laden, on He sped
For me.

Pierced through His hands and feet,
Three hours there on Him beat
Fierce rays of noontide heat
For me.

Thus wast Thou made all mine:
Lord, make me wholly Thine:
Grant grace and strength divine
To me.

JOHN LONG

Between the Seasons

To watch the snow melt and fade away,
To feel the warmth of a morning sun.
To know that winter has had its day
And the long-awaited Spring has now begun.

The wind that blew those kites to heights untold
Has given way to breeze of gentle heat.
The beauty of the rose doth now unfold
And in the meadow sheep graze in pastures sweet.

Oh shall that sultry sun go down at last,
Oh hasten not the closing of the day.
Those balmy days that once we knew are past
And busy hands have gathered in the hay.

Oh can you see the frost o'er fields of white
Or count the snowflakes as they gently fall.
The apples and the nuts are long full ripe
Oh think of Him Whose hand is over all.

RICHARD MCCOUBREY

Blest Cross

Thus far did I come laden with my sin;
Nor could aught ease the grief that I was in
Till I came hither: What a place is this!
Must here be the beginning of my bliss?
Must here the Burden fall from off my back?
Must here the strings that bound it to me crack?
Blest Cross! Blest Sepulchre! Blest rather be
The Man that there was put to shame for me.

JOHN BUNYAN

Bold Infidelity

Bold infidelity; turn pale and die.
Beneath this stone four sleeping infants lie;
Say, are they lost or saved?
If death's by sin they sinned for they are here,
If Heaven's by works in Heaven they can't appear.
Reason, ah, how depraved!
Turn to the Bible's sacred page, the knot's untied.
They died, for Adam sinned;
They live, for Jesus died.

Epitaph on a tombstone over four
children, in St. Andrews Church Yard,
Scotland

Borrowed

They borrowed a bed to lay His head
When Christ the Lord came down;
They borrowed the ass in the mountain pass
For Him to ride to town;
But the crown He wore
And the cross He bore
Were His own.

He borrowed the bread when the crowd He fed
On the grassy mountain side;
He borrowed the dish of broken fish
With which He satisfied;
But the crown He wore
And the cross He bore
Were His own.

He borrowed the ship in which to sit
To teach the multitude;
He borrowed the nest in which to rest,
He had never a home so rude;
But the crown He wore
And the cross He bore
Were His own.

He borrowed a room on the way to the tomb
The Passover lamb to eat;
They borrowed the cave; for Him a grave;
They borrowed the winding sheet.
But the crown He wore
And the cross He bore
Were His own.

The thorns on His head were worn in my stead,
For me the Saviour died.
For guilt of my sin the nails drove in
When Him they crucified;
Though the crown He wore
And the cross He bore
Were His own--
They rightly were mine.

L.M. HOLLINGSWORTH

Child of My love, Fear Not the Unknown Morrow

Child of My love, fear not the unknown morrow,
Dread not the new demand life makes of thee;
Thy ignorance doth hold no cause for sorrow
Since what thou knowest not is known to Me.

Thou canst not see today the hidden meaning
Of My command, but thou the light shall gain;
Walk on in faith, upon My promise leaning,
And as thou goest all shall be made plain.

One step thou seest – then go forward boldly,
One step is far enough for faith to see;
Take that, and thy next duty shall be told thee,
For step by step thy Lord is leading thee.

Stand not in fear thy adversaries counting,
Dare every peril, save to disobey;
Thou shalt march on, each obstacle surmounting,
For I, the Strong, will open up the way.

Wherefore go gladly to the task assigned thee,
Having My promise, needing nothing more
Than just to know, where'er the future find thee,
In all thy journeying I go before.

AUTHOR UNKNOWN

Cissie in Heaven

I have no little playmate
For Cissie is gone away
Far above the bright blue sky
To Jesus' home, they say.
She told me she would go
To dwell with Him in heaven
Where all the little children are
Whose sins are all forgiven.

WRITTEN BY A FELLOW SUNDAY SCHOOL
PUPIL ON CISSIE'S DEATH*

* Editor's note: Cissie was my grandmother's sister. She
died during the 1918/1919 Spanish Flu pandemic.
During the pandemic, my grandmother lost her
mother, two sisters, two cousins and her uncle. This
poem was recited at the Butterlump Sunday School
prizegiving (near Portavogie, Co. Down), when
Cissie would have been due to receive a prize.

Dedication

He left His glory-circled throne
Midst heaven's purest light,
To make this world His fleshly home,
A world of sin and night.

He left it all, not seeking crown,
Nor diadem so fair,
But seeking men by sin cast down
And sunken in despair.

If He be God and died for me,
To take away my sin,
No sacrifice too great can be
For me to make for Him.

WILLIAM (BILL) PEARCE MCCHESNEY*

*Martyred in Congo, November 25, 1964 aged 28.
See also the poem "My Choice."

Five Minutes After I Die

Loved ones will weep o'er my silent face,
Dear ones will clasp me in sad embrace,
Shadows and darkness will fill the place,
Five minutes after I die?

Faces that sorrow I will not see,
Voices that murmur will not reach me,
But where, oh, where will my spirit be,
Five minutes after I die?

Quickly the years of my life have flown,
Gathering treasures I thought my own,
There I must reap from the seed I have sown
Five minutes after I die.

Naught to repair the good I lack,
Fixed to the goal of my chosen track,
No room to repent, no turning back,
Five minutes after I die.

Now I can stifle convictions stirred,
Now I can silence the Voice oft heard,
Then the fulfilment of God's sure Word,
Five minutes after I die.

Mated for aye with my chosen throng,
Long is eternity, O, so long,
Then woe is me if my soul be wrong,
Five minutes after I die.

O, what a fool—hard the word, but true,
Passing the Saviour with death in view,
Doing a deed I can ne'er undo,
Five minutes after I die.

If I am flinging a fortune away,
If I am wasting salvation's day
"Just is my sentence," my soul shall say,
Five minutes after I die.

God help you to choose! Your eternal state
Depends on your choice, you dare not wait;
You must choose now; it will be too late
Five minutes after you die.

Author Unknown

Footprints in the Sand

One night I dreamed a dream.
As I was walking along the beach with my Lord.
Across the dark sky flashed scenes from my life.
For each scene, I noticed two sets of footprints in
the sand,
One belonging to me and one to my Lord.

After the last scene of my life flashed before me,
I looked back at the footprints in the sand.
I noticed that at many times along the path of my
life,
especially at the very lowest and saddest times,
there was only one set of footprints.

This really troubled me, so I asked the Lord about
it.
"Lord, You said once I decided to follow You,
You'd walk with me all the way.
But I noticed that during the saddest and most
troublesome times of my life,
there was only one set of footprints.
I don't understand why, when I needed You the
most, You would leave me."

He whispered, "My precious child, I love you and
will never leave you,
Never, ever, during your trials and testings.
When you saw only one set of footprints,
It was then that I carried you."

Author Unknown

Forgiven

Not far from New York, in a cemetery lone,
Close guarding its grave, stands a simple
headstone,
And all the inscription is one word alone—
Forgiven.

No sculptor's fine art hath embellish'd its form,
But constantly there, through the calm and the
storm,
It beareth this word from a poor fallen worm—
Forgiven.

It shows not the date of the silent one's birth,
Reveals not his frailties, nor lies of his worth,
But speaks out the tale from his few feet of earth—
Forgiven.

The death is unmention'd, the name is untold,
Beneath lies the body, corrupted and cold,
Above rests his spirit, at home in the fold—
Forgiven.

And when from the heavens the Lord shall
descend,
This stranger shall rise and a glorious end,
Well-known and befriended to sing without end—
Forgiven.

Author unknown

24

Gadara, A.D. 31

Rabbi, begone! Thy powers
Bring loss to us and ours.
Our ways are not as Thine.
Thou lovest men, we— swine.
Oh, get You hence, Omnipotence,
And take this fool of Thine!
His soul? What care we for his soul?
What good to us that Thou hast made him whole,
Since we have lost our swine?

And Christ went sadly.
He had wrought for them a sign
Of Love, and Hope, and Tenderness divine;
They wanted— swine.
Christ stands without your door and gently
knocks;
But if your gold, or swine, the entrance blocks,
He forces no man's hold— He will depart,
And leave you to the treasures of your heart.

No cumbered chamber will the Master share,
But one swept bare
By cleansing fires, then plenished fresh and fair
With meekness, and humility, and prayer.
There will He come, yet, coming, even there
He stands and waits, and will no entrance win
Until the latch be lifted from within.

JOHN OXENDAM

Gethsemane

Come, all ye Chosen Saints of God,
That long to feel the cleansing Blood,
In pensive Pleasure join with me,
To sing of sad Gethsemane.

Gethsemane the Olive Press!
(And why so call'd, let angels guess)
Fit Name! Fit Place! Where Vengeance strove,
And grip'd and grappled hard with Love.

'Twas here the Lord of Life appear'd,
And sigh'd, and groan'd, and pray'd and fear'd;
Bore all incarnate God could bear,
With Strength enough— and none to spare.

The Pow'rs of hell united press'd,
And squeez'd His Heart, and bruiz'd His Breast.
What dreadful Conflicts rag'd within,
When Sweat and Blood forc'd thro the Skin!

Dispatch'd from Heaven an Angel stood,
Amaz'd to find Him bath'd in Blood;
Ador'd by Angels, and obey'd;
But lower now than Angels made.

He stood to strengthen, not to fight;
Justice exacts its utmost Mite.
This Victim Vengeance will pursue;
He undertook, and must go through.

Three favor'd Servants left not far,
Were bid to wait and watch the War.
But Christ withdrawn, what Watch to keep!
To shun the Sight, they sunk in Sleep.

Backwards and forwards thrice He ran,
As if he sought some Help from Man;
Or wish'd at least they would condole
('Twas all they could) His tortur'd Soul.

Whate'er He sought for, there was none;
Our Captain fought the Field alone;
'Soon as the Chief to Battle led,
That Moment ev'ry Soldier fled.

Mysterious Conflict! Dark Disguise!
Hid from all Creature's piercing Eyes.
Angels astonish'd view'd the Scene,
And wonder yet what all could mean.

Oh, Mount of Olives! sacred Grove!
Oh, Garden, Scene of tragic Love!
What bitter Herbs thy Beds produce!
How rank their Scent! How harsh their Juice!

Rare Virtues now those Herbs contain:
The Sav'our suck'd out all their Bane.
My Mouth with these if Conscience cram,
I'll eat them with the Paschal Lamb.

Oh, Kedron, gloomy Brook, how foul
Thy black polluted Waters roll!
No Tongue can tell (but some can taste)
The Filth that into thee was cast.

In Eden's Garden, there was Food
Of ev'ry kind for Man, while good;
But banish'd thence, we fly to Thee,
O Garden of Gethsemane.

Joseph Hart

God Meant It Unto Good

"God meant it unto good"– O blest assurance,
Falling like sunshine all across life's way,
Touching with Heaven's gold earth's darkest storm
clouds,
Bringing fresh peace and comfort day by day.

'Twas not by chance the hands of faithless brethren
Sold Joseph captive to a foreign land;
Nor was it chance which, after years of suffering,
Brought him before the monarch's throne to stand.

One Eye all-seeing saw the need of thousands,
And planned to meet it through that one lone soul;
And through the weary days of prison bondage
Was working towards the great and glorious goal.

As yet the end was hidden from the captive,
The iron entered even to his soul;
His eye could scan the present path of sorrow,
Not yet his gaze might rest upon the whole.

Faith failed not through those long, dark days of
waiting,
His trust in God was recompensed at last,
The moment came when God led forth his servant
To succour many, all his sufferings past.

"It was not you but God, that sent me hither,"
Witnessed triumphant faith in after days;
"God meant it unto good," no "second causes"
Mingled their discord with his song of praise.

"God means it unto good" for thee, beloved,
The God of Joseph is the same today;
His love permits afflictions strange and bitter,
His hand is guiding through the unknown way.

Thy Lord, who sees the end from the beginning,
Hath purposes for thee of love untold.
Then place thy hand in His and follow fearless,
Till thou the riches of His grace behold.

There, when thou standest in the Home of Glory,
And all life's path ties open to thy gaze,
Thine eyes shall see the hand which now thou trustest,
And magnify His love through endless days.

Freda Hanbury Allen

Thanks be unto God for His unspeakable gift.

2 CORINTHIANS 9v15

God's Christmas Gift

He did not use a silvery box
Or paper green and red.
God laid His Christmas Gift to you
Within a manger bed.

No silken cord was used to bind
The Gift sent from above,
'Twas wrapped in swaddling cloths and bound
In cords of tender love.

There was no evergreen to which
His precious Gift was tied.
Upon a bare tree on a hill
His Gift was hung.... and died.

'Twas taken down from off the tree
And laid beneath the sod
But death itself could not destroy
The precious Gift of God.

With mighty hand He lifted Him
From out the stony grave
Forevermore for everyman
A living Gift He gave.

Author unkown

Adapted by Ricky McCoubrey

Good Friday

Am I a stone, and not a sheep,
That I can stand, O Christ, beneath Thy cross,
To number drop by drop Thy blood's slow loss,
And yet not weep?
Not so those women loved
Who with exceeding grief lamented Thee;
Not so fallen Peter, weeping bitterly;
Not so the thief was moved;
Not so the Sun and Moon
Which hid their faces in a starless sky,
A horror of great darkness at broad noon –
I, only I.
Yet give not o'er,
But seek Thy sheep, true Shepherd of the flock;
Greater than Moses, turn and look once more
And smite a rock.

Christina Rossetti

Great Expectations

What do I hope to find, should death o'ertake me;
Or, better still, to meet Him in the air?
Should Master's voice or trumpet call awake me,
What view within the heavenly mansions fair?

I know the blessèd Son of God will greet me,
With scenes of earth for me for ever past;
He delegates no other one to meet me,
When heaven's portals then I reach at last.

I'll view in wonderment the fields of Glory,
And breathe the uncontaminated air;
Not now the blighted scenes of sin's sad story,
But greatest pleasures from His hand to share.

Heaven's angel chorus chants a song of victory,
Another soul from Satan's realm brought in;
Participant in God Jehovah's mystery,
Redeemed and ransomed from the power of sin.

I'll find no tears, no pain on that fair morning,
Nor night, nor death and all its kindred woes.
I'll find no curse or sin, but all will gladden,
To leave for ever all the earthly woes.

Then, farewell earth with all your transient
pleasures,
I'll happy be with Christ, Who dwells on high.
I've more in Him than all earth's boasted treasures,
Eternally secure, above the sky.

JAMES PATERSON

Harden Not Your Heart

There is a time, I know not when,
A place, I know not where,
Which marks the destiny of men
To heaven or despair.

There is a line by us not seen
Which crosses every path,
The hidden boundary between
God's patience and His wrath.

To cross that limit is to die,
To die, as if by stealth.
It may not pale the beaming eye,
Nor quench the glowing health.

The conscience may be still at ease,
The spirits light and gay;
That which is pleasing still may please,
And care be thrust away.

But on that forehead God hath set
Indelibly a mark,
By man unseen, for man as yet
Is blind and in the dark.

And still the doomed man's path below
May bloom like Eden bloomed.
He did not, does not, will not know,
Nor feel that he is doomed.

He feels, he sees that all is well,
His every fear is calmed.
He lives, he dies, he wakes in hell,
Not only doomed, but damned.

Oh, where is that mysterious bourn,
By which each path is crossed,
Beyond which God himself hath sworn
That he who goes is lost?

How long may men go on in sin?
How long will God forbear?
Where does hope end, and where begin
The confines of despair?

One answer from those skies is sent,
"Ye who from God depart,
While it is called today, repent,
And harden not your heart."

AUTHOR UNKNOWN

Hast Thou No Scar?

Hast thou no scar?
No hidden scar on foot, or side, or hand?
I hear thee sung as mighty in the land,
I hear them hail thy bright ascendant star;
Hast thou no scar?

No wound? No scar?
Yet as the Master shall the servant be,
And pierced are the feet that follow Me;
But thine are whole; can he have followed far
Who hath no wound, no scar?

Amy Carmichael

He Called Me Out

He called me out,
The man with garments dyed
I knew His voice— my Lord, the Crucified.
He showed Himself, and oh, I could not stay;
I had to follow Him, had to obey.

It cast me out—this world, when once it found
That I within my rebel heart had crowned
The Man it had rejected, spurned, and slain;
Whom God in wondrous power has raised to
reign.

And so we are 'without the camp'— my Lord and I.
But oh, His presence sweeter is than any earthly
tie,
Which once I counted greater than His claim:
I'm 'out' not only from the world, but 'to His
Name.'

HARRY BELL

He Maketh No Mistake

My Father's way may twist and turn,
My heart may throb and ache,
But in my soul I'm glad I know,
He maketh no mistake.

My cherished plans may go astray,
My hopes may fade away,
But still I'll trust my Lord to lead
For He doth know the way.

Though night be dark and it may seem
That day will never break;
I'll pin my faith, my all in Him,
He maketh no mistake.

There's so much now I cannot see,
My eyesight's far too dim;
But come what may, I'll simply trust
And leave it all to Him.

For by and by the mist will lift
And plain it all He'll make,
Through all the way, though dark to me,
He made not one mistake.

A.M. OVERTON

He Shall Bear the Glory

Sing to God, my spirit, sing!
Joyful praise and worship bring!
He whom sinners mocked as King —
He shall bear the glory.

He in lowly guise who came,
Bore the spitting and the shame;
His the highest place and name
He shall bear the glory.

He who wept above the grave,
He who stilled the raging wave,
Meek to suffer, strong to save,
He shall bear the glory.

He who Sorrow's pathway trod,
He that every good bestow'd—
Son of Man, and Son of God,
He shall bear the glory.

He who bled with scourging sore,
Thorns and scarlet meekly wore;
He who every sorrow bore
He shall bear the glory.

Monarch of the smitten cheek,
Scorn of both the Jew and Greek,
Priest and King, divinely meek—
He shall bear the glory.

Where the thorn-wreath pressed His brow
Sits the priestly mitre now;
With the many, crowns, O how
He shall bear the glory

On the rainbow circled throne
'Mid the myriads of His own—
Nevermore to weep alone,
He shall bear the glory.

Man of slighted Nazareth—
King who wore the thorny wreath—
Son obedient unto death
He shall bear the glory.

His the grand "eternal weight";
His the priestly-regal state;
Him the Father maketh great—
He shall bear the glory.

He who died to set me free;
He who lives and loveth me;
He who comes—whom I shall see;
Jesus only, only He—
He shall bear the glory.

WILLIAM BLANE

I Cannot But God Can

I cannot but God can, Oh balm for all my care!
The burden that I drop, His hand will lift and bear.
Though eagle pinions tire, I walk where I once ran,
This is my strength to know, I cannot, but He can.

I see not but God sees; Oh all sufficient light!
My dark and hidden way to Him is always bright.
My strained and peering eyes may close in restful
ease,
And I in peace may sleep; I see not but He sees.

I know not but God knows; Oh blessed rest from
fear!
All my unfolding days to Him are plain and clear.
Each anxious puzzled "Why?" from doubt and
dread that grows,
Finds answer in this thought: I know not, but He
knows.

Annie Johnson Flint

I Followed the Saviour

In fancy I followed the Saviour,
I travelled the path that He trod,
I Found Him in faithful obedience,
Fulfilling the sweet will of God.

I walked to the room where the supper
For twelve and the Master were made;
I heard Him in sorrow inform them
How soon He's to be sadly betrayed.

I listened to voices commingled
In chanting the sad parting hymn;
I watched while the solemn procession
Went forward by moonlight so dim.

They moved to the garden of sorrows,
And three entered in with Him there;
Their eyelids grew heavy while watching,
As Jesus was broken in prayer.

I entered the hall of His judgment,
Where Pilate by Rome was enthroned;
How fierce were the cries for His bloodshed—
The Saviour the world had disowned.

I followed Him next to Golgotha,
But how can a human portray
The scene on the Mount of Redemption,
Where sins were all carried that day.

I covered my eyes but the impact
That came from the sight of the tree,
Deep humbled my soul in contrition,
For there He was dying for me.

I'll linger at Calvary's mountain,
I'll cherish the Lamb that was slain,
I'll serve Him with prayerful devotion,
Till heaven at last I shall gain.

S. FRANKLIN LOGSDON

We tarry a moment at Bethlehem.
We tarry for ever at Calvary.

JOSEPH PARKER

In Hoc Signo

The kingdoms of the earth go by
In purple and in gold;
They rise, they triumph, and they die,
And all their tale is told.

One Kingdom only is divine,
One banner triumphs still;
Its King, a Servant, and its sign
A gibbet on a hill.

G.F. Bradby

In the Crucible

Out from the mine and the darkness,
Out from the damp and the mold,
Out from the fiery furnace,
Cometh each grain of gold,
Crushed into atoms and levelled
Down to the humblest dust,
With never a heart to pity,
With never a hand to trust.
Molten and hammered and beaten,
Seemeth it ne'er to be done.
Oh! for such fiery trial,
What hath the poor gold done?
Oh! 'twere a mercy to leave it
Down in the damp and the mold;
If this is the glory of living,
Then better be dross than gold.
Under the press and the roller,
Into the jaws of the mint,
Stamped with the emblem of freedom
With never a flaw or a dint;
Oh! what a joy, the refining
Out of the damp and the mold!
And stamped with the glorious image,
Oh, beautiful coin of gold!

Author Unknown

I Said to the Man Who Stood at the Gate of the Year

I said to the man who stood at the gate of the year,
"Give me a light that I may tread safely into the
unknown";
And he replied, "Go out into the darkness, and put
your hand into the hand of God.
That shall be to you better than a light, and safer
than a known way."

So I went forth, and finding the hand of God, trod
gladly into the night.
He led me towards the hills and the breaking of
day in the lone east. So heart, be still!
What need our human life to know if God hath
comprehension? In all the dizzy strife of things,
both high and low, God hideth his intention. God
knows. His will is best.

The stretch of years which wind ahead, so dim to
our imperfect vision, are clear to God. Our fears
are premature. In Him all time hath full provision.
Then rest; until God moves to lift the veil from
our impatient eyes, when, as the sweeter features
of life's stern face we hail, fair beyond all surmise,
God's thought around His creatures our minds
shall fill.

Minnie Haskins

I See Myself Now

I see myself now at the end of my journey;
My toilsome days are ended.
I am going now to see that head which was
crowned with thorns,
And that face which was spit upon for me.
I have formerly lived by hearsay and faith,
But now I go where I shall live by sight,
And shall be with Him in whose company I
delight myself.
I have loved to hear my Lord spoken of;
And wherever I have seen the print of His shoe in
the earth,
There I have coveted to set my foot too.
His name to me has been as a civet-box;
Yea, sweeter than all perfumes.
His voice to me has been most sweet;
And His countenance I have more desired
Than they that have most desired the light of the
sun.
His word I did use to gather for my food,
And for antidotes against my faintings.
He has held me, and has kept me from mine
iniquities;
Yea, my steps hath he strengthened in his way.

JOHN BUNYAN

Little White Seed of Christian Love

Little white seed of Christian love
Cast in a pagan ground
From you shall spring a Power profound
Winning the hearts of all around
Your fearless zeal His vict'ry sound.

So came the Babe of Bethlehem
Into a world as wild;
So, in a manner meek and mild
Dwelt among men the Kingly Child
And so rejected died.

He taught that harvest can be reaped
If seed is sown and dies;
That love is shown in sacrifice;
That deepest grief to God-filled skies
Shall bring its victory.

We may not shrink from death and pain
If we the world for Him would gain;
We kneel and sing His praise
Oh God Who gavest Thine own Son,
Is this the way Thy work is done?
Always to give what costs us most,
Always to serve nor count the cost.

To give oneself is duty weighed;
To give one's child makes one afraid
For all the pain they may endure;
Though we may know the road is sure
We may not shield them from their hour –
We needs must trust them to Thy power.

O give them grace in time of need
To be from every danger freed
Secure in Thy great love.

E.M. Roseveare*

   * Written by Lady Roseveare on Christmas 1964, on
receiving word that her daughter Dr. Helen Roseveare
(a missionary in the Congo) was missing presumed
killed.

Low at Thy feet, Lord Jesus

Low at Thy feet, Lord Jesus,
This is the place for me;
Here I have learned deep lessons:
Truth that has set me free.
Free from myself, Lord Jesus,
Free from the Ways of men;
Chains of thought that have bound me
Never can bind again.
None but Thyself, Lord Jesus,
Conquered this wayward will,
But for Thy love constraining,
I had been wayward still.

Found in the Bible of John Nelson
Darby after his death

My Choice

I want my breakfast served at "Eight,"
With ham and eggs upon the plate.
A well-broiled steak I'll eat at "One,"
And dine again when day is done.

I want an ultra-modern home
And in each room, a telephone;
Soft carpets, too, upon the floors,
And pretty drapes to grace the doors.

A cozy place of lovely things,
Like easy chairs with innersprings,
And then I'll get a small TV—
Of course, "I'm careful what I see."

I want my wardrobe, too, to be
Of neatest, finest quality,
With latest style in suit and vest.
Why shouldn't Christians have the best?

But then the Master I can hear,
In no uncertain voice, so clear,
"I bid you, come and follow Me,
The lowly Man of Galilee.

"Birds of the air have made their nest,
And foxes in their holes find rest;
But I can offer you no bed,
No place have I to lay My head."

In shame I hung my head and cried.
How could I spurn the Crucified?
Could I forget the way He went,
The sleepless nights in prayer He spent?

For forty days without a bite,
Alone He fasted, day and night.
Despised, rejected—on He went,
And did not stop till veil was rent.

A Man of sorrows and of grief,
No earthly friend to bring relief—
"Smitten of God," the prophet said—
Mocked, beaten, bruised, His blood ran red.

If He be God and died for me,
No sacrifice too great can be
For me, a mortal man, to make;
I'll do it all for Jesus' sake.

Yes, I will tread the path He trod,
No other way will please my God;
So henceforth, this my choice shall be,
My choice for all eternity.

WILLIAM (BILL) PEARCE McCHESNEY*

*Martyred in Congo, November 25, 1964 aged 28.
See also the poem "Dedication."

Only One Life

Two little lines I heard one day,
Travelling along life's busy way;
Bringing conviction to my heart,
And from my mind would not depart;
Only one life, 'twill soon be past,
Only what's done for Christ will last.

Only one life, yes only one,
Soon will its fleeting hours be done;
Then, in 'that day' my Lord to meet,
And stand before His Judgment seat;
Only one life, 'twill soon be past,
Only what's done for Christ will last.

Only one life, the still small voice,
Gently pleads for a better choice
Bidding me selfish aims to leave,
And to God's holy will to cleave;
Only one life, 'twill soon be past,
Only what's done for Christ will last.

Only one life, a few brief years,
Each with its burdens, hopes, and fears;
Each with its claims I must fulfil,
Living for self or in His will;
Only one life, 'twill soon be past,
Only what's done for Christ will last.

When this bright world would tempt me sore,
When Satan would a victory score;
When self would seek to have its way,
Then help me Lord with joy to say;
Only one life, 'twill soon be past,
Only what's done for Christ will last.

Give me Father, a purpose deep,
In joy or sorrow Thy word to keep;
Faithful and true what e'er the strife,
Pleasing Thee in my daily life;
Only one life, 'twill soon be past,
Only what's done for Christ will last.

Oh let my love with fervour burn,
And from the world now let me turn;
Living for Thee, and Thee alone,
Bringing Thee pleasure on Thy throne;
Only one life, 'twill soon be past,
Only what's done for Christ will last.

Only one life, yes only one,
Now let me say, "Thy will be done";
And when at last I'll hear the call,
I know I'll say "twas worth it all";
Only one life, 'twill soon be past,
Only what's done for Christ will last.

C.T. Studd

Fear not: for I have redeemed thee,
I have called thee by thy name;
thou art mine.
When thou passest through the waters,
I will be with thee;
and through the rivers,
they shall not overflow thee:
when thou walkest through the fire,
thou shalt not be burned;
neither shall the flame kindle upon thee.

ISAIAH 43v1-2

Passing Through

"When thou passest through the waters,"
Deep the waves may be and cold,
But Jehovah is our refuge,
And His promise is our hold;
For the Lord Himself has said it,
He, the faithful God and true;
"When you come unto the waters
You will not go down, but through."

Seas of sorrow, Seas of trial,
Bitter anguish, fiercest pain,
Rolling surges of temptation
Sweeping over heart and brain...
They will never overflow us
For we know His work is true;
All His waves and all His billows
He will lead us safely through.

Threatening breakers of destruction,
Doubt's insidious undertow,
Will not sink us, will not drag us
Out to ocean depths of woe;
For His promise will sustain us,
Praise the Lord, whose word is true!
We will not go down, or under,
For He says, "You will pass through."

Annie Johnson Flint

Resignation

A little bird I am,
Shut from the fields of air,
And in my cage I sit and sing
To Him who placed me there;
Well pleased a prisoner to be,
Because, my God, it pleaseth Thee.

Nought have I else to do,
I sing the whole day long;
And He whom most I love to please
Doth listen to my song;
He caught and bound my wandering wing;
But still He bends to hear me sing.

Thou hast an ear to hear
A heart to love and bless;
And though my notes were e'er so rude,
Thou wouldst not hear the less;
Because Thou knowest as they fall,
That love, sweet love, inspires them all.

My cage confines me round;
Abroad I cannot fly;
But though my wing is closely bound,
My heart's at liberty;
For prison walls cannot control
The flight, the freedom of the soul.

O it is good to soar
These bolts and bars above!
To Him whose purpose I adore,
Whose providence I love;
And in Thy mighty will to find
The joy, the freedom of the mind.

MADAM GUYON
(TRANSLATOR UNKNOWN)

She Has Chosen the World

She has chosen the world,
And its paltry crowd,—
She has chosen the world,
And an endless shroud!
She has chosen the world,
With its misnamed pleasures;
She has chosen the world,
Before Heaven's own treasures.

She hath launched her boat
On life's giddy sea,
And her all is afloat
For eternity;
But Bethlehem's Star
Is not in her view;
And her aim is far
From the harbour true.

When the storm descends
From an angry sky,
Ah! Where from the winds
Shall the vessel fly?
When stars are concealed,
And rudder gone,
And Heaven is sealed
To the wandering one!

The whirlpool opes
For the gallant prize;
And, with all her hopes,
To the deep she hies!
But who may tell
Of the place of woe,
Where the wicked dwell—
Where the worldings go?

For the human heart
Can ne'er conceive
What joys are the part
Of them who believe;
Nor can justly think
Of the cup of death
Which all must drink
Who despise the faith.

Away, then— O, fly
From the joys of earth!
Her smile is a lie—
There's a sting in her mirth.
Come, leave the dreams
Of this transient night,
And bask in the beams
Of an endless light.

Robert Murray McCheyne

"*Yes*", said Queen Lucy,
"in our world too, a stable
once had something in it that
was bigger than our world."

C.S. LEWIS
(THE LAST BATTLE)

That Night

That night when in the Judean skies
The mystic star dispensed its light,
A blind man moved about in sleep—
And dreamed that he had sight.

That night when shepherds heard the song
Of hosts angelic choiring near,
A deaf man stirred in slumber's spell—
And dreamed that he could hear!

That night when in the cattle stall
Slept Child and mother cheek by jowl,
A cripple turned his twisted limbs—
And dreamed that he was whole.

That night when o'er the newborn Babe
The tender Mary rose to lean,
A loathsome leper smiled in sleep—
And dreamed that he was clean.

That night when to the mother's breast
The little King was held secure,
A harlot slept a happy sleep —
And dreamed that she was pure!

That night when in the manger lay
The Sanctified who came to save,
A man moved in the sleep of death—
And dreamed there was no grave.

Author unknown

The Advent

The sphere was ready; letters, laws, and might
Had reared a lofty structure for the light
The world still needed; while on Zion's hill
Faith waited for Jehovah to fulfil
His ancient promise, Fears like shadows fell,
Oh! Could it be that God Himself would dwell
With men on earth? Was Bethlehem to be
The lowly scene of a nativity
In glory so transcendent? Would He come
The Prince of Peace, and make with us His home?
Then suddenly on swift and silent wing
Sped Gabriel the blissful news to bring

That He was coming, heralded by one,
Like the bright star before the rising sun;
For Judah was remembered, and the word
Of old to Abraham spoken by the Lord
And thou, O Virgin blest of Israel's race,
On thee the singular and sacred grace
Was shed, that through thy travail should be born,
The Saviour King, whose coming, like the morn,
Should bring the sons of sorrow sweet release,
And guide our feet into the way of peace.

Methinks I hear the music of that night
At Bethlehem, when on the shepherds' sight
There shone the angelic vision, and the sound
Of seraphs' singing swept the earth around!
What joy it wakes! What wonder and amaze,
Glory To God In Heaven, And Highest Praise,
On Earth Peace, Divine Good Will To Men!
And still it echoes as it echoed then;
The willing air prolongs each cadence sweet,
The hills and valleys listen and repeat
Each blest refrain, with joy again;
To You Is Born A Saviour, Christ The Lord
All hail the welcome word! This is the morn
The world has waited for - To You Is Born
A Saviour! Let it thrill
The raptured ear - A Saviour! sound it still;
It is the angels who the song upraise,
On Earth Be Peace And Unto God Be Praise!

And Thou, the King of glory, in Thy love
Didst then descend from radiant world above
To dwell in this, and men beheld Thy face
Bedewed with pity, and adorned with grace;
And from Thy lips the words immortal fell
The sorrowful, the weary love so well.
And Thou didst found a Kingdom by the might
Of truth, by deeds of love, and arms of light;
And still its triumphs spread, and still they tower
Sustained by Thine imperishable power.
Oh! Man of Sorrows, in Thy robe of scorn,

How well became Thy brow its wreath of thorn!
What riches in Thy poverty and loss!
What everlasting glories in Thy cross!
Thou didst refuse a kingdom, from a crown
Didst turn away; Divine Thou camest down
From heaven, Thyself in all things to abase,
To ransom and to raise a ruined race.
Yet Caesar knew thee not, Tiberius heard
No sentence of Thy wonder-working word,
Nor dreamed the Roman that a King was born,
Whose stroke should shiver every Gentile horn.

How great the contrast - in empurpled state
Sits Caesar; On his bidding thousands wait;
The earth its treasure at his feet hath spread -
But Jesus hath not where to lay His head.
Beneath the stars, beneath the midnight dew,
The lonely desert was the home He knew;
Or where the olive, with the foliage spare,
Gave shelter from the chilly mountain air.
Though at His bidding winds and waves were still,
Though earth and heaven but waited on His will,
Yet all for us He wandered in the wild,
Of pain the heir, of poverty the child.
O never did there bloom beneath the skies
So fair a flower as this; nor mortal eyes
Behold the perfect loveliness of grace,
Without a shadow - save in Jesus' face.

And still the olive grows upon the steep
Where Jesus stooped to worship and to weep
And in the rustle of its foliage sage
Seems softly whispering of a bygone age:
A tree of lowly, unpretending mien,
Adorned but simply in the sunny scene,
Yet strangely useful; from the stony soil
Extracting precious food and priceless oil.
A tree whose fruit, like goodness in distress,
Is bruised for man beneath the heavy press:
A grateful shade by day and in the night
A generous spring to feed the constant light.
Oh, marvel not that He who all things made
Should love when here on earth the olive shade;
Yea wonder not its lowly form to see
In sweet and sorrowful Gethsemane.

O Conqueror Crucified, Thy loss is gain,
The travail triumph; power is in Thy pain;
Thy mortal weakness is Thy matchless might,
Self Immolation of the Infinite!
No words, O love divine, can language find
To speak Thy measure or express Thy mind;
Our mortal love is cast in narrow mould;
Born of the earth, 'tis limited and cold,
Yea, poor and strengthless when compared with this,
That stooped from heaven to print its healing kiss
Upon man's fevered brow, to breathe its peace,
And bring the world forgiveness and release.

O thou refulgent flaming Eye of day,
Drooping thy lid of darkness and dismay,
And you, ye rending Rocks, and opening Graves,
Well may ye own the mighty One who saves,
While hanging helpless on the accursed tree;
Your High and sovereign Potentate is He,
Never in might more mighty than this hour,
Dying, victorious o'er destruction's power!

For God so loved the world that He hath given
The sons of Earth His only Son in Heaven,
The brightness of His glory, in whose face
Shines most express the image of His grace;
By whom He made the worlds, and doth sustain
Their order: who to bear the cross did deign;
And having purged our sins, Himself alone
By His great sacrifice, upon the throne
Sat down and rested as a glorious King,
Waiting in Heaven till Providence shall bring
His foes to be His footstool. On His breast
He bears His people's names; by Him expressed
Before the Father's face are all their needs,
Whose love delights to listen while He pleads.

The blushing flower the solar beam receives,
Embracing light; 'tis thus the heart believes.
Or as the earth drinks in the blessed rain
Which on its bosom falleth not in vain;
So welcomes faith the sweet celestial truth;
Revived, inspired, the soul regains its youth;
No more it shrinks in ignorance and gloom,
No longer dreads the coming day of doom;
Mercy extends the shelter of her wing,
And Hope looks up, and hears the angels sing!

Henry Grattan Guinness

The Anvil of God's Word

Last eve I paused beside the blacksmith's door,
And heard the anvil ring the vesper chime;
Then looking in, I saw upon the floor,
Old hammers, worn with beating years of time.

"How many anvils have you had," said I,
"To wear and batter all these hammers so?"
"Just one," said he, and then with twinkling eye,
"The anvil wears the hammers out, you know."

And so, I thought, the Anvil of God's Word
For ages skeptic blows have beat upon;
Yet, though the noise of falling blows was heard,
The Anvil is unharmed, the hammers gone.

ATTRIBUTED TO JOHN CLIFFORD

The Burial of Moses

By Nebo's lonely mountain,
On this side Jordan's wave,
In a vale in the land of Moab,
There lies a lonely grave.
But no man dug that sepulchre,
And no man saw it e'er;
For the angels of God upturned the sod,
And laid the dead man there.

That was the grandest funeral
That ever passed on earth;
But no man heard the trampling,
Or saw the train go forth.
Noiselessly as the daylight
Comes when the night is done,
And the crimson streak on ocean's cheek
Grows into the great sun—

Noiselessly as the springtime
Her crest of verdure weaves,
And all the trees on all the hills
Open their thousand leaves—
So, without sound of music,
Or voice of them that wept,
Silently down from the mountain crown
The great procession swept.

Perchance some bald old eagle
On gray Beth-peor's height,
Out of his rocky eyrie
Looked on the wondrous sight.
Perchance some lion, stalking,
Still shuns the hallowed spot,
For beast and bird have seen and heard
That which man knoweth not.

But when the warrior dieth
His comrades in the war,
With arms reversed and muffled drums
Follow the funeral car;
They show the banners taken,
They tell his battles won,
And after him lead his matchless steed
While peals the minute gun.

Amid the noblest of the land
They lay the sage to rest;
And give the bard an honoured place,
With costly marble drest,
In the great minister's transept height,
Where lights like glory fall,
While the sweet choir sings and the organ rings
Along the emblazoned wall.

This was the bravest warrior
That ever buckled sword;
This the most gifted poet
That ever breathed a word;
And never earth's philosopher
Traced, with his golden pen,
On the deathless page, truths half so sage
As he wrote down for men.

And had he not high honour?
The hillside for his pall;
To lie in state while angels wait
With stars for tapers tall;
And the dark rock pines, like tossing plumes,
Over his bier to wave;
And God's own hand, in that lonely land,
To lay him in his grave.

In that deep grave without a name,
Whence his uncoffined clay
Shall break again – most wondrous thought!—
Before the judgment day,
And stand, with glory wrapt around,
On the hills he never trod,
And speak of the strife that won our life
Through Christ, the incarnate God.

O lonely tomb in Moab's land,
O dark Beth-peor's hill,
Speak to these curious hearts of ours,
And teach them to be still.
God hath His mysteries of grace—
Ways that we cannot tell;
He hides them deep, like the secret sleep
Of him he loved so well.

Mrs. C.F. Alexander

The Care of God

The God Who marks the sparrow's fall,
Who clothes the lily on the lea,
And heeds the hungry raven's call—
Such is the God Who cares for me.

A peace divine e'en now is mine,
From every care my heart is free;
What need I fear when Christ is near,
Or dread while God does care for me?

Though heaven's glory is His shrine,
Where all before Him bow the knee,
A place in His great heart is mine—
Who knows my needs and cares for me.

Revolving worlds His wisdom guides;
He rules in heaven, and earth, and sea,
Yet in His great pavilion hides
A weak and worthless thing like me.

Should I His tender care forget,
Or cease His guiding hand to see,
His heart is so upon me set,
He ceases not to care for me.

Thus I am happy all the day,
My soul is filled with heavenly glee,
My only care Him to obey,
Who ever loves and cares for me.

WILLIAM BLANE

*He shall gather
the lambs
with His arm,
and carry them
in His bosom.*

ISAIAH 40v11

The Folded Lamb

Rest for the little sleeper!
Joy for the ransomed soul!
Peace for the lonely weeper,
Dark tho' the waters roll.

Weep for the little sleeper:
Weep, it will ease thy heart,
Tho' the dull pain be deeper
Than with the world to part.

Mighty the conflict o'er him!
How could he face the foe?
Rugged the road before him!
How could the weak one go?

He could not climb the mountain;
He could not face the foe,
Lying between Life's Fountain,
And this dark vale below.

But the kind Shepherd found him,
Laid him upon His breast,
Folded His arms around him,
Hushed him to endless rest.

He bore him up the mountain,
He trampled down the foe,
He laid him by Life's Fountain,
Whence the still waters flow.

Joy for the little sleeper,
The gentle, timid lamb,
Safe with his tender Keeper!
Could there be sweeter balm?

Oh! what are earth's best pleasures,
Sick'ning the woe-struck heart?
What all its joys and treasures,
When with the loved we part?

But the long-wished-for token,
Earnest of peaceful rest,
Binds up the heart that's broken,
Soothes the distracted breast.

Do not, then, droop in sadness,
Dark tho' the night may be;
There's a bright morn of gladness,
Mourner, reserved for thee!

Grieve not with hopeless sorrow,
Jesus has felt thy pain;
Thy child He did not but borrow,
He'll bring him back again.

Peace, little loving sleeper,
Close to the Saviour's side,
Housed with thy tender Keeper,
Safe—for "the Lord has died!"

Author unknown

The Little Birds of God

 I hear them at my window in the late, gray winter
dawn,
The little birds of God, the farthing sparrows of
His care;
They ask of me, as I of Him, His gift of daily
bread.
With soft, impatient twitterings they voice their
morning prayer.

The heavenly Father feedeth them, the little birds
of God,
Though 'tis my hand that scattereth the food
within their reach;
I do but share His bounty when I give the crumbs
to them.
Doubting heart and anxious heart, what lessons
they can teach!

They sow not, neither do they reap, nor gather into
barns,
Content if but each day shall bring the day's supply
of food;
No question whence it comes, nor if the morrow
bringeth more
Small optimists in feathers, who are sure that all is
good!

God seeth when they fly or fall. Am I less worth
than they?
I would not fail them in their need. Is He less true
than I?
I would not mock their faith in me, nor hurt them,
nor betray;
I answer to their trusting call, He to His children's
cry.

When sunset tints the fading light and dusk is
falling fast,
The while I draw the curtains close and stir the
hearth-fire bright,
I hear their cheerful chirping, the little birds of
God,
And wonder to what shelter they are fleeing for the
night.

But they, as I, shall rest secure beneath the wings of
Love,
Though storm and darkness sweep the sea and
cover all the land.
My life and theirs, so small and frail, God's care of
both the same;
My soul a nesting bird within the hollow of His
hand.

Annie Johnson Flint

The Maker of the Universe

The Maker of the universe
As Man, for man, was made a curse.
The claims of Law which He had made,
Unto the uttermost He paid.

His holy fingers made the bough,
Which grew the thorns that crowned His brow.
The nails that pierced His hands were mined
In secret places He designed.

He made the forest whence there sprung
The tree on which His body hung.
He died upon a cross of wood,
Yet made the hill on which it stood.

The sky that darkened o'er His head,
By Him above the earth was spread.
The sun that hid from Him its face
By His decree was poised in space.

The spear which spilled His precious blood
Was tempered in the fires of God.
The grave in which His form was laid
Was hewn in rocks His hands had made.

The throne on which He now appears
Was His for everlasting years.
But a new glory crowns His brow
And every knee to Him shall bow.

F.W. PITT

The Man in the Glory

I wake in the morning with thoughts of His love
Who is living for me in the glory above,
In glad hope awaiting till He calls me away,
And that keeps me bright as I go day by day;
But the moments speed forward, and on comes the
noon,
Yet still I am singing, "He'll come very soon;"
And thus I am watching from morning to night,
More than they who desire to see the daylight

There's a Man in the glory I know very well,
I have known Him for years, and His goodness can
tell;
One day, in His mercy, He knocked at, my door,
And, seeking admission, knocked many times o'er;
But when I went to Him, and stood face to face,
And listened awhile to His story of grace,—
How He suffered for sinners, and put away sin,—
I heartily, thankfully, welcomed Him in.

We have lived on together a number of years,
And that's why I have neither doubtings nor fears.
For my sins are all hid in the depths of the sea;
They were cast away there by the Man on the tree.
I am often surprised why the lip should be curled,
When I speak of my Lord to the man of the world,
And notice with sorrow his look of disdain
When I tell him that Jesus is coming again.

He seems so content with his houses and gold,
While despising the Ark, like the people, of old;
And yet at His coming I'm sure he would flee,
Like the man in the garden, who ate of the tree.
I cannot but think it is foolish of souls
To put all their money in "bags that have holes,"
To find, in the day that is coming apace,
How lightly they valued the "riches of grace."

As fond as I am of His work in the field,
I would let go the plow, I would lay down the
shield
The weapons of service I would put on the shelf,
And the sword in its scabbard, to be with Himself;
But I'll work on with pleasure, while keeping my
eyes
On the end of the field, where standeth the prize.
I would work for His glory, that when we shall
meet,
I may have a large sheaf to lay down at His feet,

That He too with pleasure His fruit may review.
Is the Man in the glory a stranger to you?
A stranger to Jesus? What! Do you not know
He is washing poor sinners much whiter than
snow?
Have you lived in a land where the Bible's
unknown
That you don't know the Man Who is now on the
throne?
Ah, did you but know of His beauty and power,
You would not be a stranger another half-hour.

I have known Him so long that I am able to say,
The very worst sinner He'll not turn away.
The question of sin, I adoringly see,
The Man in the glory has settled for me!
And as to my footsteps, whatever the scene,
The Man in the glory is keeping me clean;
And therefore I'm singing, from morning to night,
The Man in the glory is all my delight.

GEORGE CUTTING

The Proper Way

"The proper way for a man to pray,"
Said Deacon Lemuel Keys,
"The only proper attitude
Is down upon his knees."

"No, I should say, the way to pray,"
Said Reverend Doctor Wise,
"Is standing straight with outstretched arms
And rapturous upturned eyes."

"It seems to me his hands should be
Devoutly clasped in front,
With both thumbs pointing t'ward the ground,"
Said Reverend Doctor Blunt.

"Last year I fell in Hodgkin's well
Head first," said Cyrus Brown.
"With both my heels a'sticking up,
My head a'pointing down.

And I made a prayer right then and there,
Best prayer I ever said—
The prayerest prayer I ever prayed
Was standing on my head."

Author unknown

Fear ye not, therefore;
you are of more value
than many sparrows.

MATTHEW 10v31

The Robin and the Sparrow

Said the robin to the sparrow,
"I should really like to know,
Why these anxious human beings
Rush about and worry so."
Said the sparrow to the robin,
"Friend I think that it must be,
That they have no Heavenly Father,
Such as cares for you and me."

Elizabeth Cheney

The Schools of Scribes

The schools of scribes and courts of kings,
The learn'd and great He passes by.
Chooses the weak and foolish things,
His power and grace to testify;
Plain simple men His call endues
With power and wisdom from above;
And such He still vouchsafes to use,
Who nothing know but Jesus' love.

CHARLES WESLEY

The Sea of Galilee

How pleasant to me thy deep blue wave,
O sea of Galilee!
For the glorious One who came to save
Hath often stood by thee.

Fair are the lakes in the land I love,
Where pine and heather grow;
But thou hast loveliness far above
What Nature can bestow.

It is not that the wild gazelle
Comes down to drink thy tide,
But he that was pierced to save from hell
Oft wandered by thy side.

It is not that the fig-tree grows,
And palms, in thy soft air,
But that Sharon's fair and bleeding Rose
Once spread its fragrance there.

Graceful around thee mountains meet,
Thou calm reposing sea;
But ah! Far more, the beautiful feet
Of Jesus walked o'er thee.

These days are past – Bethsaida, where?
Chorazin, where art thou?
His tent the wild Arab pitches there
The wild reeds shade thy brow.

Tell me, ye mouldering fragments, tell,
Was the Saviour's city here?
Lifted to heaven, has it sunk to hell,
With none to shed a tear?

Ah! Would my flock from thee might learn
How days of grace will flee;
How all an offered Christ who spurns,
Shall mourn at last, like thee.

And was it beside this very sea,
The new-risen Saviour said
Three times to Simon, "Lovest thou me?
My lambs and sheep, then feed."

O Saviour! Gone to God's right hand!
Yet the same Saviour still,
Graved on thy heart is this lovely strand
And every fragrant hill.

Oh! give me, Lord, by this sacred wave,
Threefold Thy love divine,
That I may feed, till I find my grave,
Thy flock – both thine and mine

ROBERT MURRAY MCCHEYNE

The Shell

Upon the sandy shore an empty shell,
Beyond the shell infinity of sea;
O Saviour, I am like that empty shell;
Thou art the Sea to me.

A sweeping wave rides up the shore, and, lo,
Each dim recess the coiled shell within
Is searched, is filled, is filled to overflow
By water crystalline.

Not to the shell is any glory then:
All glory give we to the glorious sea.
And not to me is any glory when
Thou overflowest me.

Sweep over me, Thy shell, as low I lie,
I yield me to the purposes of Thy will;
Sweep up, O conquering waves, and purify.
And with Thy fulness fill.

AMY CARMICHAEL

The Touch of the Master's Hand

'Twas battered and scarred, and the auctioneer
Thought it scarcely worth his while
To waste much time on the old violin,
As held it up with a smile.
"What am I bidden, good folks," he cried;
"Who'll start the bidding for me?"
"A dollar, a dollar. Then two! Only two?
Two dollars, and who'll make it three?"

"Three dollars, once; three dollars, twice;
Going for three…" But no,
From the room, far back, a grey-haired man
Came forward and picked up the bow;
Then wiping the dust from the old violin,
And tightening the loosened strings,
He played a melody pure and sweet,
As a caroling angel sings.

The music ceased, and the auctioneer,
With a voice that was quiet and low,
Said: "What am I bid for the old violin?"
And he held it up with the bow.
"A thousand dollars, and who'll make it two?
Two thousand! And who'll make it three?
Three thousand, once; three thousand, twice,
And going and gone," said he.

The people cheered, but some of them cried,
"We do not quite understand.
What changed its worth?" Swift came the reply:
"The touch of the Master's hand."
And many a man with his life out of tune,
And battered and scarred with sin,
Is auctioned cheap to the thoughtless crowd
Much like the old violin.

A "mess of pottage," a glass of wine,
A game — and he travels on.
He is "going" once, and "going" twice,
He's "going" and almost "gone."
But the Master comes, and the foolish crowd
Never can quite understand
The worth of a soul and the change that is wrought
By the touch of the Master's hand.

Myra Brooks Welch

The Weaver

My Life is but a weaving
Between my Lord and me,
I cannot choose the colours
He worketh steadily.

Oft times He weaveth sorrow
And I in foolish pride
Forget He sees the upper
And I, the underside.

Not till the loom is silent
And the shuttles cease to fly
Shall God unroll the canvas
And explain the reason why.

The dark threads are as needful
In the Weaver's skillful hand
As the threads of gold and silver
In the pattern He has planned.

He knows, He loves, He cares;
Nothing this truth can dim.
He gives the very best to those
Who leave the choice to Him.

GRANT COLFAX TULLAR

The Widow's Mite

Two mites, two drops (yet all her house and land),
Falls from a steady heart, though trembling hand.
The other's wanton wealth foams high, and brave,
The other cast away, she only gave.

RICHARD CRASHAW

The Young Christian

I cannot give it up,
The little world I know!
The innocent delights of youth,
The things I cherish so!
'Tis true, I love my Lord
And want to do His will,
And oh! I may enjoy the world,
And be a Christian still!

I love the hour of prayer,
I love the hymns of praise,
I love the blessed Word that tells
Of God's redeeming grace.
But I am human still!
And while I dwell on earth
God surely will not grudge the hours
I spend in harmless mirth!

These things belong to youth,
And are its natural right—
My dress, my pastimes, and my friends,
The merry and the bright.
My Father's heart is kind!
He will not count it ill
That my small corner of the world
Should please and hold me, still!

And yet— "outside the camp"
'Twas there my Saviour died!—
It was the world that cast Him forth,
And saw Him crucified.
Can I take part with those
Who nailed Him to the tree?
And where His name is never praised
Is there the place for me?

Nay, world! I turn away,
Though thou seem fair and good;
That friendly outstretched hand of thine
Is stained with Jesus' blood.
If in thy least device
I stoop to take a part,
All unaware, thine influence steals
God's presence from my heart.

I miss my Saviour's smile
Whene'er I walk thy ways;
Thy laughter drowns the Spirit's voice,
And chokes the springs of praise.
If e'er I turn aside
To join thee for an hour,
The face of Christ grows blurred and dim
And prayer has lost its power!

Farewell! Henceforth my place
Is with the Lamb Who died,
My Sovereign! While I have Thy love
What can I want beside?
Thyself, dear Lord, art now
My free and loving choice,
"In whom, though now I see Thee not,
Believing, I rejoice!"

Shame on me that I sought
Another joy than this,
Or dreamt a heart at rest with Thee
Could crave for earthly bliss!
These vain and worthless things,
I put them all aside;
His goodness fills my longing soul,
And I am satisfied.

Lord Jesus! let me dwell
"Outside the camp," with Thee!
Since Thou art there, then there alone
Is peace and home for me.
Thy dear reproach to bear
I'll count my highest gain,
Till thou return, my banished King,
To take Thy power, and reign!

Margaret Mauro

They on the Heights

They on the heights are not the souls
Who never erred nor went astray.
Or reached those high rewarding goals
Along a smooth, flower-bordered way.
Nay, they who stand where first comes dawn,
Are those who stumbled – but went on.

J. Sidlow Baxter

Thirty pieces of Silver

Thirty pieces of silver,
For the Lord of life they gave
Thirty pieces of silver,
Only the price of a slave;
But it was the priestly value,
Of the Holy One of God.
They weighed it out in the temple,
The price of the Saviour's blood.

Thirty pieces of silver,
Laid in Iscariot's hand;
Thirty pieces of silver,
And the aid of an armed band,
Like a lamb that is led to the slaughter,
Brought the humble Son of God,
At midnight from the garden,
Where His sweat had been like blood.

Thirty pieces of silver,
Burns on the traitor's brain;
Thirty pieces of silver,
Oh it is hellish gain:
I have sinned and betrayed the guiltless,
He cried with a feverish breath
And he cast them down in the Temple,
And rushed to a mad man's death.

Thirty pieces of silver,
Lay in the house of God,
Thirty pieces of silver,
But oh 'Twas the price of blood;
And so for a place to bury,
The strangers in they gave
The price of their own Messiah,
Who lay in a borrowed grave.

It may not be for silver,
It may not be for gold,
But still by tens of thousands,
Is this precious Saviour sold.
Sold for a godless friendship,
Sold for a selfish aim,
Sold for a fleeting trifle,
Sold for an empty name,
Sold in the mart of science,
Sold in the seat of power,
Sold at the shrine of fortune,
Sold in pleasures bower?

Sold where the awful bargain,
None but God can see,
Ponder my Soul the question,
Shall He be sold by thee?
Sold? O God what a moment?
Stifled in consciences' voice
Sold? But the price of the Saviour,
To a living coal shall turn,
With the pangs of remorse forever,
Deep in the soul shall burn.

WILLIAM BLANE

Time to Pray

I got up early one morning
And rushed right into the day;
I had so much to accomplish
That I didn't have time to pray.

Problems just tumbled about me,
And heavier came each task.
"Why doesn't God help me?" I wondered.
He answered, "You didn't ask."

I wanted to see joy and beauty,
But the day toiled on, gray and bleak;
I wondered why God didn't show me.
He said, "But you didn't seek."

I tried to come into God's presence;
I used all my keys at the lock.
God gently and lovingly chided,
"My child, you didn't knock."

I woke up early this morning,
And paused before entering the day;
I had so much to accomplish
That I had to take time to pray.

AUTHOR UNKNOWN

Upon Thy Word I Rest

Upon the Word I rest,
Each pilgrim day;
This golden staff is best
For all the way.
What Jesus Christ hath spoken
Cannot be broken!

Upon the Word I rest,
So strong, so sure;
So full of comfort blest,
So sweet, so pure!
The charter of salvation,
Faith's broad foundation,

Upon the Word I stand!
That cannot die!
Christ seals it in my hand,
He cannot lie!
The Word that faileth never!
Abiding Ever!

Frances Ridley Havergal

Weeping Olivet

King David, God's rejected man,
Crossed o'er the brook and wept.
Forsaken by his own, he climbed
Up weeping Olivet.

Another king, his greater Son,
While all the city slept,
In perfect manhood prayed to God
On weeping Olivet.

In Bethany, He groaned and cried,
While friends their vigil kept,
His voice which raised the dead was heard
At weeping Olivet.

The city of His God He viewed,
With sorrow and regret.
"I would, but they would not," He mused,
From weeping Olivet.

Into the garden soft He went,
A little further yet.
Bowed to His God, sweat drops as blood
On weeping Olivet.

Beside each mountain that He made,
A valley He did set.
Into the valley He must go,
From weeping Olivet.

The enemy was waiting there,
The battle to be met.
Forward He went and won the day,
From weeping Olivet.

To Zion's mountain He'll ascend,
And many sons beget.
He'll never be alone again
On weeping Olivet.

His feet shall stand and split the mount
In glorious triumph yet,
And living waters then shall flow
From singing Olivet.

O glorious Lord, on Whom around
Such glory is beset,
As living stones we'll sing Thy praise
Like singing Olivet.

No sorrow then shall cross Thy brow,
No tears Thy face shall wet.
Heaven and earth shall sing Thy praise,
And singing Olivet.

Surrounded by Thy seed they'll sing
The valley ne'er forget;
Nor toil nor tears, nor groans nor blood,
Nor weeping Olivet.

Ricky McCoubrey

What are the Wounds?

He sits on the throne which is ever His own,
And heavenly hosts He commands;
He gives us each hour His grace and His power—
But what are the wounds in His hands?

He is coming some day in glorious array,
To wield control of all lands,
With triumph assured through sufferings
endured—
But what are the wounds in His hands?

All kindreds shall wail, no foe shall prevail,
As victor on earth He then stands;
All war shall e'er cease as he proffers His peace—
But what are the wounds in His hands?

From heaven to earth in lowliest birth,
He came to loosen death's bands;
He went to the cross and suffered great loss,
And there got the nails in His hands.

He grappled with sorrow, no help could He
borrow,
Yet met all the legal demands;
He cried, "It is done!" as the vict'ry was won,
But still had the wounds in His hands.

The price that He paid and the peace that He made,
The whole of my life now commands;
But when heaven I gain, with the saints there to reign,
He'll still have the wounds in His hands.

S. Franklin Logsdon

How unspeakably wonderful to know that all our concerns are held in hands that bled for us.

JOHN NEWTON

What God Hath Promised

God hath not promised skies always blue,
Flower-strewn pathways all our lives through;
God hath not promised sun without rain,
Joy without sorrow, peace without pain.

God hath not promised we shall not know
Toil and temptation, trouble and woe;
He hath not told us we shall not bear
Many a burden, many a care.

God hath not promised smooth roads and wide,
Swift, easy travel, needing no guide;
Never a mountain, rocky and steep,
Never a river, turbid and deep.

But God hath promised strength for the day,
Rest for the labourer, light for the way,
Grace for the trials, help from above,
Unfailing sympathy, undying love.

Annie Johnson Flint

When God Wants to Drill a Man

When God wants to drill a man and thrill a man
and skill a man,
When God wants to mold a man to play the
noblest part;
When He yearns with all His heart to create so
great and bold a man
That all the world shall praise…watch His
methods; watch His ways!

How He ruthlessly perfects whom He royally
elects…
How He hammers him and hurts him and the
mighty blows converts him
Into frail shapes of clay that only God understands.
How his tortured heart is crying and he lifts
beseeching hands…
How He bends but never breaks, when his good
He undertakes,
How He uses whom He chooses…with every
purpose fuses him;
By every art induces him to try His splendour
out…
God knows what He's about.

J. Oswald Sanders*

* (Adapted from a poem by Angela Morgan)

Whether I Live or Die

Lord, it belongs not to my care,
Whether I die or live;
To love and serve Thee is my share,
And this Thy grace must give.

If life be long I will be glad,
That I may long obey;
If short–yet why should I be sad
To soar to endless day?

Christ leads me through no darker rooms
Than He went through before;
He that unto God's kingdom comes,
Must enter by this door.

Come, Lord, when grace has made me meet
Thy blesséd face to see;
For if Thy work on earth be sweet,
What will Thy glory be!

Then I shall end my sad complaints,
And weary, sinful days;
And join with the triumphant saints,
To sing Jehovah's praise.

My knowledge of that life is small,
The eye of faith is dim;
But 'tis enough that Christ knows all,
And I shall be with Him.

RICHARD BAXTER

Wise Men

Wise men travelled from afar
To worship at His feet.
The heavens rang when angels sang
And shepherds left their sheep.

And so He beckons to our hearts,
To worship, serve and sing;
And think of Him Who came to die,
And heartfelt gifts to bring.

Ricky McCoubrey

Wounded for My Transgressions

Wounded for my transgressions!
Slowly the words I read:
Swiftly the tears will gather,
Truly the heart should bleed.

Wonderful condescension!
Matchless, infinite grace!
Jesus, the Sinless, — Holy, —
Taking the sinner's place.

Wonderful, wonderful story!
Wonderful depth of love!
Laying aside His glory,
Leaving the courts above;

Jesus, the Man of sorrows,
Homeless and friendless, He,
Wounded — so cruelly wounded, —
Bruised — and broken — for me.

Fiercely the storm sweeps round Him!
Darkly the shadows fall;
Wrath, and anger, and judgment, —
Jesus — bearing it all;

Draining the cup of anguish,
Dying on Calv'ry's tree:
Wondrous plan of redemption: —
Jesus — dying — for me!

Author unknown

Index by Title

Index of First Lines